HUMAN GPS

GOD'S PERFECT SCRIPT

JANET PALMER

HUMAN GPS

GOD'S PERFECT SCRIPT

THE FULFILLMENT OF MY WHY

PEACH PUBLISHING

This book is designed to provide information that the author believes to be accurate on the subject matter it covers, and is written from the author's personal experience. In the text that follows, many people's and company's names and identifying characteristics have been changed, so that any resemblance to actual persons, living or dead, events, companies or locales is entirely coincidental.

Any references to resources and materials produced by other entities are purely the author's own interpretation. The author does not imply an endorsement from any of the sources cited within this book.

ISBN 978-0-473-47320-4 (PAPERBACK)

Human GPS — God's Perfect Script:
The Fulfillment of My Why

First Printing, 2019
Peach Publishing
createnonfiction.com

To my parents, Noel and Daisy,
who provided the rich, fertile environment
that made the gestation of these thoughts
possible.

To God,
for the many gifts that I've received
throughout my life. Be they human or not,
all have contributed to the creation of these
words.

To my brother, John,
who taught me lessons I have yet to fully
embody.

To Ben,
for your love and support during this entire
process.

A Quick Note From Janet:

Throughout this book, I will orient you to the fulfillment of your Why, much like how a Global Positioning System does. Namely, you will be asked to identify who you are, to collect data regarding your current surroundings, as well as to note where you are going. Examples and techniques will be provided to clarify the process as you go along.

CONTENTS

INTRODUCTION

THE FIRST 'WHY'

I was about three years old when my parents got that phone call from the doctor, the doctor who ultimately confirmed that, yes, my little brother John would be diagnosed as mentally retarded.

My parents were broken. I sat on the floor of our house, aware of their grieving, and additionally aware of my brother playing off to the side. I came to a sudden, vivid decision: *That's okay,* I thought, *I'll take care of him.*

In retrospect, that event was the first evidence of my Why—the first moment I evinced my reason for being. From then on I took John under my wing. From the seat of my being, throughout my childhood and beyond, I did everything I could to include him in every way possible. Even though it began as a self-imposed responsibility, John and I quickly became inseparable. All my life choices were guided and decided according to how I'd include my brother.

We grew up as a preacher's kids, and in sermon after sermon I heard the same message:

We are designed for a purpose.

We are all unique. We each offer something that no one else can. As my understanding of that truth deepened, my commitment to caring for John moved from just responsibility to purpose: I expressed my Why in caring for John. It expressed the reason I was created.

My Why guided me and worked for me. It helped me to understand that part of my purpose is to inspire altruism. Embracing the concept also freed me to examine other things that interested and excited me. Everything aligned when I saw my life this way—me in light of my Why. My life had an organizing principle.

An outline, as it were, was before me, an outline in the shape of me, a space where I felt true to myself.

Nothing felt out of place. I discovered that when I am truly aligned and moving in step with my Why, the rhythm of my life is unforced. I need not rely on willpower. A sense of purpose stands ready to fuel me. In living my Why, I live out the true me, and being truly me becomes the most natural thing in the world. It's empowerment, it's energy, it's a power pack that I never have to go pick up or recharge because it resides within me. The same is true for everyone and anyone who lives in their Why.

Though taking in sermons fanned the spark of my Why, I'm not saying you must believe in my vision of God to achieve this. At least, though, be confident that somebody or something larger than you created you. For me, that's God; God is my creator.

When I accepted Him as my creator and embarked upon an active and growing relationship with Him, I also found that my Why got clearer and clearer. Meanwhile, the deeper my relationship became, the freer I felt to live in my Why.

I knew the peace and joy of a life not filled with the strife of striving. I could enjoy the gifts this world provides in sunsets, birds singing, snow falling, and the diversity of people that crossed my path. I saw the promise of people empowered to do things that they never thought to do previously. I understood myself as one empowered to do things that I might have never thought to do until it was my purposed time to do them.

Critics have said that at times I have been selfish because I let nothing interfere with me living my

Why. In reality, though, my Why was the highest gift I could give to my community.

I desire to give my all, to spend myself, all of myself, until there is nothing left unused. Giving this way is satisfaction—God created me for this, after all. I can only realize myself to the fullest by spending my most valuable currency— me—and I won't leave anything in reserve.

Living my Why is my chance to play a role that only I can fulfill. It is my chance to inspire and empower my community, perhaps in amazing ways. No act by any of us occurs in a vacuum:

> *By fully investing in my Why, touching the lives of others, I nourish them and feed their Whys in turn.*

This ultimately comes back to me, and I am nourished. When you spend from your Why, you complete cycles of life and in so doing, feel complete.

FACING THE UNKNOWN

I met my current husband at 49-years-old after working 22 years in a job as a school psychologist. I lived in New York; he lived in Texas. We got married, and it was easier for me to move to Texas than for him to move to New York.

Prior to meeting him, I'd been trying my darnedest to find a job as an administrator for a school district. I wanted to be involved in the making of policies that would give a voice to the children I served. I never got offered a position. Interview after interview, I ended up as one of two finalists—only to not land the job. This didn't happen just a handful of times; this happened for years. It was maddening. I have an administrative degree that I've never used— or should I say, not used *yet!*

So, when my husband asked me to move to Texas, I decided the time had come for me to leave the school district. Though I had no second thoughts, my supporters voiced anxiety.

"Janet", they said, "There's no closure! You're interrupting your service! Your pension is not going to be maxed! And, you're not retiring?

"You're leaving the place you've lived for most of your life. You are leaving your family. You're leaving with this man you just met—how do you even know the marriage is going to work?! You will have no support system there. All you will have is this man and his children—in his hometown!"

My reply was always "God and one is a majority, so I am good."

That decision, thanks to my Why—a decision many would find difficult—was a no-brainer for me.

My job hadn't been fulfilling me for some time. For years, I'd been trying without success to get a new one. The route to fulfilling my Why on that path was blocked.

Moving felt more like a purposeful opportunity than a loss. The decision was made easy because I felt confident in my purpose instead of being full of uncertainty. Sure, there were questions I didn't have the answers to, but my Why acted as a bright light showing me which way to go.

And let's not forget my relationship and trust in my creator, my savior. My faith sustained me: Again, God and one is a majority. I felt, and still feel, empowered by His presence! God doesn't lose track of His children and what they're up to. He didn't wake up the day of my decision and say, "Whoops, uh, where's Janet? I'm looking for Janet. Where is she?" None of this took Him by surprise.

Stumbling and fumbling along are not how He works. In creating me He also created a purpose for me, and these events were a part of His plan.

TRAFFIC AHEAD

There are times as a parent when you know beforehand what your kids will do, right? Sometimes what they're about to do is blatantly obvious, even if the paths they're taking aren't clear to them.

This also happens in my walk with God except I am the child. Yet, the more I surrender and trust, the more insight I gain and the more ability I have to let Him guide me. Just as a wise child might stop and look to Mom or Dad for clues and signals of approval or warning, I look to God.

When I'm living in my Why, remaining in His presence, there's a GPS within me that navigates and brings me back to the proper course. At times this navigation system can even report that there's trouble on the road ahead.

When I trust my Why—God's Perfect Script (GPS) for me—when I trust it, the GPS throws needed light on my way.

PREPARED TO WALK IN THE LIGHT

A quote in a sermon from T.D. Jakes goes like this:

> *"You never rise to a situation; you only go to the level of your preparation."*

That truth played out at the point in my life when my parents and brother needed a lot of care, so much that I had to return to New York. I didn't "rise to the occasion" of their caregiving. Rather, I functioned within my level of preparedness: I'd been created to serve, so caring for people was a purpose for which I'd been practicing my whole life in more ways than I knew.

That circumstances called me back to New York made sense. It even, in an interesting way, comforted me because being a caregiver was nothing new. I had what it took because my life's journey had prepared me and led up to this. I could see the events, circumstances, and detours of my life as confirmation for such times.

The night before my dad died, he started drilling me about certain matters: *Janet, what do you do if this happens? What if that happens? What if this and that happen? What do you do?*

My father was trying to ensure I'd be okay and prepared for whatever might come. I didn't know at the time that this would be one of our last conversations, but it was. He died the next morning. Dad was gone.

Now I was left to care for Mom and my brother John. New territory, but again, it held no surprises for God. All I had to do was trust. Comfort came from knowing I could rely on Him to navigate as I walked through these new chapters of my life.

Strength emerged as I practiced my Why within the framework of my relationship with God. I followed it, I trusted it. Updates on my path's "road conditions" came through—warning signs, five-minute traffic jams, detours. I was truly living and relying on my GPS.

Meanwhile, Mom missed Dad tremendously, after all, they were married for almost 60 years. She was dealing with loss and grief, all while medical complexities added to her difficult times. Fortunately, I'd been prepared for this, too. Way back in my early twenties, my then husband and I ran recreational trips for developmentally disabled adults. The skills learned during that time, as well as my training in psychology, enabled me to help Mom navigate her new life circumstances.

I felt empowered, drawing upon the experiences provided by my creator for such a time as this, and it went well. Mom could truly enjoy the last two-and-a-half years of her life after Dad passed.

Even on familiar roads I use God's Perfect Script for my life. He navigates me. I see delays as times he uses to make me aware of His presence.

So, whether my path runs straight and smooth or turns dark and bumpy, I can adjust and re-orient by using my navigational system with total assurance that my course has been charted by Him and that there's a purposeful path.

COACHING VS. PSYCHOLOGY

Many of my most fulfilling client coaching sessions have taken place very late at night. I know that sounds odd, but usually that's when people need the most support. They're alone, they can't sleep, they've either drank themselves to oblivion or have used narcotics, and they're in a place of darkness. It's dark outside and there's darkness inside, and they don't feel like they can call anybody else.

After I make sure that someone in that situation is safe and not in imminent danger from themselves or others, we begin our dialogue. It's amazing to support people both literally and figuratively in their "dark night" experiences. It's amazing to see that switch go on both physically and figuratively at the first glimmer of sunlight. Having lived my share of dark times and moments, too, makes me able to run emotionally alongside them, to help them navigate through their dark and lonely times.

When I discovered coaching, I immediately felt drawn to it over psychology.

Coaching embraces people where they are. It accepts the fact that people are doing the best they can, even when they're not doing what's best.

Although that might not seem logical, it can be. An example of this is someone *knowing* that eating a balanced diet and exercising is the best thing medically, but not doing it until they suffer a heart attack. Bolstered by that, they suddenly have the impetus to instantly change direction.

Coaching not only meets people where they are, but even better, it empowers them for where they're going. This makes coaching much more congruent with what I lived and saw in my parents' treatment of my brother John. And most of all, coaching resonated with my Why.

So, I pursued coaching as my new career. I took courses and became certified, and then in my private then-psychology practice, I transitioned my clients to coaching. I asked them to take this journey with me, and they were wonderful enough to agree. Interestingly, some commented that they actually didn't see much of a difference.

Regardless, we made the transition, signed the forms, and made it legal: I wasn't their therapist anymore—I was their coach.

My focus became inspiration. My mission as a coach was to encourage clients to do the great things for which they were created.

They—like you—are masterpieces, and I want to see everybody walk in that truth.

Everyone needs to be supported on that journey. Everyone needs to be anchored, authenticated, and inspired. It doesn't matter whether it's the brightest day or the darkest night, inspiration can be yours.

REORIENT & REVITALIZE

In my day-to-day, I coach people and businesses on how to find their personal and corporate Whys.

Company A was barely holding on. They brought me in to help after they'd fallen to almost nothing.

Where once they had been soaring, now they'd lost focus and had crashed. No longer could they deliver on promises. Their employees did not support them; there was anarchy among the masses. The company not only lost their clients, they even lost their physical location. They dropped down to bare bones. An operation of 30 had been whittled to two and then to just one—the founder. Can you imagine how he must have felt?

When my team came in, we started asking questions: Why? What is this all about? Where did you lose your focus? Who are you? Let's go back to what brought you joy in the first place—why did you even decide to create this company? Should you be merging with another company or should you be on your own?

Answering those questions reoriented the company. They found their course and slowly they steadied. Things began turning around. They rehired some people, but not without asking each an important question, one vital to the company's survival and its purpose. They asked the newly hired and rehired, *What's your Why?* How is your Why congruent with your understanding of the company's Why? How can this relationship of employee and employer be beneficial to both our Whys?

The company didn't want anyone externally-driven in their relationship with the company; they wanted everyone to be internally-propelled to do better and to contribute their skills and desires to the company's purpose.

They wanted a win-win of Whys going forward, a situation where everyone involved was devoted toward the good of their common efforts, a situation where everyone was in sync.

Now revitalized, the company is expanding. By getting in step with itself, the company found its way forward.

OUT OF SYNC

When you don't know your Why, or if you know it but you're not following it, you won't feel whole. Maybe you recognize that feeling. It's common enough. Without your Why you feel incomplete, maybe even insufficient. You can't shake the feeling that you're capable of more.

During these times, feelings of undue sadness, discontent, or dis-ease creep in. Maybe these sensations don't merely creep in, but barge in! They could be pointing to the fact that you're not living in your Why.

Meanwhile, when you do live in your Why, you're not just motivated, you're inspired! There's a big difference. Leadership expert Dr. Lance Secretan explains the difference this way: Motivation comes from a place outside yourself. It is of the external world and comes to most of us by way of rewards and punishments. Inspiration, though, burns from within.

There's another distinction between motivation and inspiration: Motivation has an expiration date. Once the reward is granted or the axe of the punishment falls, there goes your motivation.

Inspiration doesn't expire. Its light keeps burning, generating a "do energy" on its own. You don't have to strap on an energy pack from outside to propel you or fuel you. Your energy pack is safe inside you, powered by the inspiration of your Why. Following your Why maximizes your energy.

Unfortunately, some of us can't even think in terms of maximizing our energy because we lost track of it long ago. Our motivation has waned. There might be times when you catch a glimpse of your desired self, maybe even experience it for a short period until the many voices within urge you to shut it down, give up, and no longer believe your desire is possible. External motivation cannot sustain you.

We try, though, searching for some external source we can put on, pull out of a toolbox, or practice. We shout aloud the right words ten times a day to boost us to the next level of desire and performance. At that level, we hope, we'll feel better; at that level we hope to feel free; at that level we hope to stimulate success. But we don't feel better or free and the hoped for success stays out of reach.

We crave that externalized fix because we don't trust ourselves to already have all we need to do what we need to do from our deepest selves.

We don't believe we are whole and complete, and we don't have faith in what our creator and savior has placed within us. It's an epidemic, this crisis of trust: We don't trust that we are created for a purpose. We don't trust our individuality and greatness. We don't trust that our ripple in the pond of life is significant. We think that only certain people—special people—are chosen to make a difference in the world. Not us, right?

I work with a lot of individuals who just feel stuck. They're going through the motions of life. They get up, go to work, come home. They get up, go to work, come home. They get up, go to work, come home... This day in and day out. They've turned their lives into life sentences.

Unfulfilling—that's how they describe their relationships. They begin to add things to their lives—alcohol, club memberships, the theater, sex, "stuff"—but these are just external compensations, a stab at fulfillment from the outside. You can lose weight, gain weight, join a club, a church, a gym, but these won't fulfill you completely or for long. Again, they're external. You can get a new job, new friends, move out of state—things won't change for long. Soon, that familiar dis-ease creeps in.

When this happens, I often tell them to look back at their childhood or to find a time in life where they felt happy and emotionally light. I ask them to consider what gave them joy. "When were you happy?" I ask them. "When were you carefree?"

I also suggest to examine your environment and surroundings. A technique adopted from Dr. Lance Secretan is to ask, "What stands out as something that needs to be adjusted or corrected? What stands out as causing pain, dissatisfaction, or distress? What would the world look like without those things?" I listen to their answers.

Another suggestion I make may seem odd. Bear with me, though: I ask, "When you see something that distresses you, what is the color or the shape or the temperature of that oppressive situation?"

Then: "What is the color, the temperature, and the shape of the solution? Where do the distress and the solution resonate in your body?"

These imaginative exercises can give you an emotional sense of release as you feel the solution. They can also open your eyes to where your Why lives and give you hope.

You will become more hopeful as you see your Why because you will realize you don't have to go out and bring something into your life to feel fulfilled or inspired—you have the source of fulfillment and inspiration within and it goes with you wherever you go. You have light within you, and by using and relying on it, you illuminate all situations that come your way.

LEARNING TO TRUST YOURSELF

Once we allow ourselves time to reflect and begin to embrace where we find ourselves in all the various places of our lives—environmentally, emotionally, physically, spirituality, and financially—we can accept things as they are. Whether things are good, bad, or ugly, we can feel a sense of belonging, enjoying the support afforded us by everything and everyone around us.

This space of belonging and being in relationship with community, nature, God, and material things bolsters you and enables movement. Traveling through your day, the car you drive allows you to be encased safely as you go from place to place. The birds you see and hear allow you to join them as they share your day. Every item, person, and situation that appears during your day has come for a purpose, and those moments empower, clarify, utilize, and challenge your Why.

The people you pass as you go about fulfilling your duties are there at that specific time to teach you something or learn something from you; they are an integral part of your Why. We all just need to be willing and open to receive from our space of belonging, to receive and live true to our Whys or to give to our current space of belonging as we grow into and live true to our Why.

For example, not long ago I was running late for an appointment. Each of my sessions had run five minutes longer than planned and there was traffic on the freeway: I would be 45 minutes late. In my car I asked myself, "How is my life and reaction to these events both now and in the future going to evidence what I support as a coach?"

I knew that in my morning calls prior to leaving the office I had provided an ear for each of my clients. Each of them had expressed deep appreciation. By living true to my Why and created purpose, I self-provided a release of anxiety and stress as I journeyed to my next appointment. I was calmed by my thoughts and could let other drivers in as they entered the freeway or needed to change lanes. One driver rolled down his window and thanked me for being so cordial.

When I parked my car and headed toward my client's office, I saw a woman ahead of me, walking with a boy of about eight. He was crying inconsolably, and she seemed to be at her wit's end. Seeing my concern, she asked if I could help. She told me he was a foster child just placed with her. When she had stopped to pick something up, the boy thought he had seen his mom.

I spoke with them for a while and he described the person he thought was his mother. I told him I was running late for an appointment, but if they would come inside with me, I would do everything I could to help.

It turned out that when we got into my client's office, the woman the boy thought was his mom was there, and he was able to see for himself that he was mistaken. They left my client's office in a much better state than they had been when I saw them initially.

Living true to my Why had cleared me to be accepting of circumstances and assured that everything worked for both my good and that of those with whom I was allowed to cross paths. Had I not been "late"—had I not been given the question to examine myself and the integrity of my being—I would not have been used to help people who were hurting and unnerved. The experience once again confirmed my Why.

From the beginning of time, we have been on a quest to discover and understand our surroundings and our purpose. As I read in the Old Testament, mankind has always desired to know more, hence the fall of Adam and Eve.

Even as we share their desire to know where we fit in this wide and unknown world, we also share an internal sense of "in the beginning."

It's part of being human, having a starting point that serves as a reference point. Adam and Eve's starting place could be seen as the garden, and everything that followed was measured against it.

We always carry our starting points with us. We use them to take stock of our nows, comparing, assessing, and reorienting to the varied and various places through which we travel.

Meanwhile, as we think back to our respective starting points, we find things unique to each one of us. Regardless of the number of people who may share similar starting places and circumstances, our particular place holds a special and unique relevance because of our personal Why. *Why* makes our starting point exclusive.

When you use the reference point of your very own beginning to take stock of your "right now", you will never—can never—end up with the same insights and discoveries as someone else.

I went to high school with a girl who, interestingly enough, was born on the same day, at around the same time, and in the same hospital as I was. Despite all those similarities, including the fact that we had ended up attending the same private school, our lives were vastly different, and because of our Whys, the significance of our overlapping circumstances meant different things to each of us. For me, the significance might be that some 44 years in the future I'd be writing a book that needed a relevant example.

Let's think about that because it's important. If you take stock and ask yourself, *what am I to do? Where am I to go? Am I doing and being all that I am meant to be?* —your answers will be unique, customized to you alone. Such questioning provides meaningful answers that can move you toward discovering and living out your Why.

Go further: If I'm here, placed in this position in between these markers, there must be a reason. Even if somebody else is standing right next to me in the same space, their markers, their references are specific to them. But what is my reason? What is the reason for me?

Finding your Why means learning how to trust yourself—to trust your individuality.

The problem is that, too often, people mistake

individuality for isolation.

Enjoying your unique self, all the events that have contributed to making you who you are, is significant. It takes time to understand, appreciate, and act on it. It means turning off outside noises, the things that distract us from a place of reflection.

Having done so, we discover a greater and more profound sense of belonging.

Instead of isolation, we find connectedness and purpose.

We have forgotten how important it is to belong, to be in relationship with a community, to interact with your GPS and the things put along the way by God when He created us. We have forgotten how to belong to Him and how to be in His presence. We often focus on the temporary external and let it reflect us rather than incorporating it into who we were created to be.

You came here for a reason, you were brought here to do something. You didn't just start at the point of impregnation. No one, I repeat no one, is a waste. You are here at such a time as this in such a place as this for a specific reason.

There is a reason. Don't you want to find out what that reason is?

1
START WITH WHERE YOU ARE

You keep doing the same things. Year after year after year, you live in that routine. Even if you are unhappy with it, the routine is part of your comfort zone. It's a well-worn path, actually more of a rut. Climbing out now would take effort, and you may fear that it could even cause an injury. So, on you plod. The days change, but the tasks don't. Now you're just going through the motions, and that has been true for a while. Does that describe you?

*If it does, are you happy on your beaten path—
truly happy?*

If you picked up this book, some part of you has likely been thinking about your Why. If so, you're in a place of questioning, and questioning is good. If you're longing for change, taking stock of the Right Now is required, and taking stock is about asking serious questions.

So far you probably know that you want change, but you're not so sure change can happen—not without somebody on the outside helping you and pushing you forward. You probably don't believe that everything you need to bring about lasting change is congregated inside you right now. If you could do this already, you wouldn't be in a rut, right?

Here's some good news: You've already started the process of change. You started when you began to honestly ask the questions you're already asking. Change begins by looking around and then investigating whatever looks like stagnation in your life. By finding the courage to really look at where you are, you have already taken the first step toward change.

More good news: you're gaining strength. Knowledge is power, as we know, and you're gaining it by asking questions. You may not see the answers to all your questions right away, but now your eyes are open, looking out for answers.

I've got a third piece of good news, a secret hidden in plain sight: You already have the most important answers to your most important questions. As you look at your world and yourself, asking the questions that can bring about the changes you crave, you'll find answers by looking inward. Insight will strengthen and empower you.

You might not have the confidence to believe these things just yet—that you already have what it takes to change, that you're already doing it, that you possess the important answers, that you're already growing stronger, and that you are, in fact, whole and complete. You're not alone in that. You belong to a world that downplays the rewards of an internalized source. External forces in our culture say that we have to acquire things outside ourselves in order to feel whole, complete, and okay. But there is no missing piece in you.

If you feel empty, it is because you're hungering— hungering for your Why, hungering to live out that Why, and hungering to live as your whole and true self.

DISCOVER YOUR ENVIRONMENT

You may have noticed on your rutted path that your routine has its own momentum, a momentum that makes it hard to stop. Even if you're going in circles, the sense of forward motion keeps you moving.

Now you'll put that phenomenon to work for you, letting your process of discovery build upon itself naturally—only this time, you actually will be getting somewhere, going somewhere, and growing. From the day that you decide there has to be more, the day you take the initiative to connect with your creator and the world you've been provided, you will start to grow.

So, let's seize this day and make it Day One!

To begin, consider a seed. When you eat an apple, a cherry, or a peach, you fling the seed, right? If you're driving along the interstate and fling that seed out the window at 60 miles per hour, there is something within that seed that, despite how it was thrown, despite where it lands, wants to grow. Growth is in its nature. As long as there's soil, sunshine, and rain, something within that seed tells it to begin germinating, and the seed obeys.

The richness of the environment wherein the seed resides will have a part in determining how successful that seed is. The seed itself doesn't mind one way or the other how fit that environment is or isn't. Even if a seed is lodged in the crack of a sidewalk between concrete slabs, it will germinate. The potential within the seed is much greater than its environment; the environment does not change a seed's innate potential. Again, growth is in its nature.

It's your nature, too. Within us is a seed, a desire for greatness—our own greatness. We have an innate desire to be fulfilled and to understand our uniqueness. That desire—our potential—is an integral part of what our wiring is about. It is a living energy that environment cannot diminish.

Though environment can affect you, it cannot
extinguish potential and the need to fulfill its—
your—nature. God made it so.

Now, please remember that environment is not just what surrounds us physically. Internally, it is your own thought processes as well as your innate desire to become all that you were created to be.

Your environment includes your social circle and the friends influencing you. Your environment might be not only your literal location but also virtual places like social media and memberships such as your place of worship or religion, your political party, and your culture.

Ask yourself, *are these things and places providing me with what I need to thrive? Or, are they just causing me to survive and remain smaller than I was created to be?*

PINPOINT YOUR LOCATION

Since you're questioning, feeling like you're in a rut, chances are the answer is no—your environments are not providing what you need to thrive. So, you must be willing to change that.

You're going to be gathering information to help you find your created direction. In the meantime, change something about what you do right now. Drive a different route to work. Change your schedule. Stay in bed longer. Get out of bed earlier. Decide to change something about your environment and follow through.

You can begin with yourself. Remember, your environment isn't only physical spaces. You can make a mental change, a physical change, or both. Perhaps you decide to look for one amazing thing every day. You might decide to cut your hair. The important thing is the willingness to adjust your environment, even if in a small way. This begins the process of getting you out of your circular rut and actually give direction to your unique potential.

The best kinds of changes come from knowing your exact starting point, so here at the beginning invest time in taking an inventory of your life. See where you are and appreciate this place. Embrace it, begin to feel a sense of perspective and wholeness.

By so doing, you will free and inspire yourself to move toward a new destination.

Don't underestimate the value of this dawning perspective. You must really understand your environment to pinpoint your exact location, just like on a GPS. The more information the GPS can gather about where you are, the clearer your route to a new location will be. If your GPS can't locate your starting point, how can it possibly guide you? It has sparse information to work with! So, take account of where you are to create that whole and complete feeling.

Foster the inspired juices within to find and be uplifted by a new perspective. Discover how fabulously the elements of your life have served you or how they have instead dis-served you and be ready to make small but significant adjustments.

Don't limit this exploration of your life to just a mere cataloguing of its features. Remember, you want to understand your life and environment. You want to understand yourself within it. Your exploration all comes back to questions. Ask yourself, *why was I created? Has my life had themes, things that keep cycling back in? What does that say about my reason for being? Am I fulfilled in what I do? Do I ever feel lost? Do I ever feel inspired? When? Why?*

You must be completely honest. All of the good, the bad, and the ugly have contributed to where you are right now. Of course these questions and answers need to be judgement-free; this is about collecting information, adding to your knowledge base, heightening your awareness—not casting judgment.

All these questions and answers aren't just preliminary work preparing you for a journey. You're actually on the journey right now, mapping and triangulating your position like a ship's captain. Time hasn't stopped and you're not standing still. Your life is moving along, but now you've started the process of getting your bearings so that you can set a truer course. Now it's time to keep it going.

2
USE YOUR PAST TO REVEAL YOUR WHY

Can you remember a time when things were easier?

I sometimes start my coaching sessions with this question. I ask clients, and now I'm asking you, when did you enjoy a time of success? When did things go well? When did you feel good about yourself?

Reflecting on such times can help us discover exactly when, how, and why it was that we enjoyed feelings of success. These answers help us understand what makes our particular successes personally meaningful. It's time for you to begin exploring my questions, uncovering the answers that will shine light on your path.

As you start looking back, it might be helpful to create a timeline to hold the insights you will find.

Now, keeping in mind your better times, start exploring:

› What were you doing when you felt good about how things were going?
› What were your days like?
› Where did you spend time?
› Who were your daily companions?
› Did you feel fulfilled? Why?

Find more questions by prompting yourself with the classic five Ws and the How of grade school essay writing. Be open to this exercise, willing to start asking and keep asking. Not only can the questioning yield crucial insights—these insights can change your future—but also, looking back to easier times can free you to feel, once again, that you do have the ability to be successful, though you seemingly have forgotten. I've seen this happen repeatedly with my clients:

Burdened with a persistent perception of doom and gloom or living out gray days of burn-out and apathy, they have forgotten themselves as successful, viable, vibrant people.

Some of these clients, entrenched in a dreary now, resist looking back. Dwelling on past successes could be problematic, they worry. They fear the pain, acknowledging that somewhere success was lost. Or they believe that this part of their past is irrelevant to the present and that looking back at times of feeling good is just an exercise in self-indulgence that won't get them anywhere.

It is an exercise, but not in self-indulgence. It's another exercise in mapping and navigation. You are finding useful reference points. Acknowledging the path that got you to where you are now will enable you to chart your course toward finding your way to your Why.

You see, if you un-anchor yourself from successful experiences, you won't have the advantage of seeing your possible future through the bright lens of a person who has real-world experience in success. Instead, gray days will color everything, dampening, darkening, and discouraging you.

In my practice, when we explore gloominess, people tend to realize that defeatist feelings cannot be trusted at face value. Defeat has become calcified, and it needs to be penetrated to see what's underneath. To break the feelings down I start with this question: Where have you actually sustained success all the way through to now?

There's always a thread of success that runs throughout life. Have you been able to maintain fitness or education? Have you consistently nourished a garden or your pets? Have you been a good daughter or son? A good sibling? Have you been good at being a good friend? Do you love God no matter the blows that life delivered your way? Thinking on these, why are you glossing over or even dismissing proof of your ability to succeed?

If you find yourself resisting this look back at success, you must challenge your resistance and then get back to looking back.

Let's start: Do you remember a time when things were easier?

TIME TRAVELING

After my clients search for and find their answers, we move forward in time to discover when they lost the feeling of success. It's your turn now to do the same. Look at your timeline and pinpoint that shift.

When did you no longer feel successful? What was the corresponding shift in your life? What happened around that time? Look at the who of that, the what of that, the when, the why, the how. Also, how did the loss of feeling successful echo forward in time? Thinking about it, how do you feel right now as you reflect on it all?

Some of you might think you have an immediate answer to when the wheels came off. Maybe a big event in your life shook your success loose and you can point to it with honest vehemence. Maybe responsibilities called for a sacrifice that hobbled you, and you haven't felt good or vital since. Even if you think you know the answers to questions about the shift away from success, still take time to reflect.

Your life is not a headline.

Reread the story of your past. New insights likely await you there.

RECOLLECTING YOURSELF TO RE-COLLECT YOURSELF

Tracing the path from past success to its loss can not only shine light on your life as a whole, but also on its parts. The spotlight can reveal places that need healing and opportunities for constructive change.

Sarah was having issues with her child. She was, as she put it, clueless about how to successfully raise him as a single mom. There was a custody issue, and she had started to say things like, "I'm no good at this... Maybe he'd be better off with his dad. After all, he's a boy."

I asked her, "What would make Dad more of a success than you?"

"Well, his gender," she responded.

"So, you're meaning to tell me that no male child has ever been successfully raised by a mom?"

"No," she admitted.

"Was there ever a time in your son's 13 years here on earth that you felt successful?" I asked.

"When he was younger," she said. But now, she explained, her son was in adolescence, and adolescence is notoriously difficult.

As we explored the situation, she began to make some connections. She realized this child of hers was dredging up memories from her own adolescence, unresolved issues of abandonment, rejection, insecurity, and others. Sarah had been 13 when her own mother sent her away to live with an aunt. Her estranged father appeared on the scene for a fleeting moment and then went off and had a new family, never to see her again for 20 years. Some of Sarah's power was dimmed by the long shadows of a past falling forward on her present.

I explored further, asking her, "What would you have liked to have had when you were a 13-year-old child? That doesn't mean that your son needs that, but it may inspire and free up something for you as his mom."

This was important homework for Sarah. She needed to reflect and be transparent with herself, journal her feelings, and email her discoveries to me. The answers, she knew, might provide the key to finding success in her current situation.

A few weeks of self-reflection later, Sarah talked with her son about what was going on and how she was feeling. The relationship between them changed drastically for the better. She could own the origins of her feelings and fears while still being able to see how equipped she was to listen and support her son the way he needed. She also could ask her son's father to provide more time so that they could balance their shared interest in their son's well-being.

> Recollection enabled Sarah to reach back into the past and re-collect her power, finding a way to succeed with her son once again.

LIVING SOMEONE ELSE'S WHY

Unhealed past injuries can steal resources you need to succeed, but what if you've just given those resources away? This is more common than you might think, often in the arena of career, a place where many of us measure our self-worth.

> Josh, a CEO who felt his life needed a totally different direction, had lost his passion; he was working outside of his Why. His true desire had been to be a salesman, but Josh thought if he ventured into law it could be more lucrative. Many of his friends and family members had pursued it and encouraged him to as well.
>
> Pursue it he did, and he was good at the work, but living incongruently with whom he truly was. The more money he made, the more dissatisfied he became. He was surviving emotionally, but not thriving. He was just plodding along. His participation in the family's law practice just didn't fulfill him. It couldn't. He wasn't created to live as a lawyer and Josh could feel it deep down in his soul.

Our sessions involved reflecting on what gave him joy. He looked for the times when he actually did feel congruent with whom he really was and what he really stood for. When Josh allowed himself to bask in whom he really was instead of living out somebody else's life or somebody else's dream or somebody else's desires for him—he found his strengths awakening. He went back to his sweet spot and began to live again, exploring ways that he could enter the sales profession and sell merchandise.

Within two months of living out his sweet spot by doing sales, Josh had tripled his earnings, regained his inspiration and joy, and felt fulfilled. He gave up someone else's Why, reclaimed his own, and by doing what he loved—what he was created to do—he gained emotional fulfillment and did extremely well financially.

ARE YOU LIVING OUT SOMEONE ELSE'S WHY?

Many times, I've heard people say they're sure—so sure—that they're living out their Why. They know what they want and they're going after it full force, they say. Unfortunately, too often these Whys aren't really *theirs*.

*They're Whys that have been imposed through
outside forces like family expectations, peer
pressure, or the allure of glamor.*

Adopting a Why from outside often happens when
people are going off to college or when they've just
completed it and need to find a job. During such
times, well-meaning family members often start
pushing for life goals they perceive as good instead
of encouraging their loved ones to follow what
really draws them from the core. Too often the
pressure works.

If you aren't clear on your Why, it's easier to take
on somebody else's concept of your best life than it is
to find your own answers. It can be hard to sit down
and look within. Grabbing hold of something offered
from someone else doesn't require the same energy
and time as self-examination.

Meanwhile, there's also pressure not to deviate
from the expectations of those around you. Everyone
wants to be in that "right" relationship with the
people they care about, so it's a risk to deviate from
expectations. The pressure can be formidable; bowing
to what's expected may seem easier. Many a person
has discovered that they lack the strength needed to
really step up and challenge those around them.

Good news: When you find your Why, when
you embrace it, when you free its voice and listen,
you can find the strength to stand up for yourself

by standing up for your Why. But first you have to find it.

FINDING YOUR WHY

Your Why speaks to you. If you have been deaf to it, it can be hard at first to catch what it's saying. You may have to listen keenly for it. Sometimes it shouts, but oftentimes your Why speaks in a still and small voice.

It's so still and small that it's easy for it to go unheard. It's not until you have declared your Why out loud that you begin to get the strength you need to silence the negativity, ignore the insecurity and ambivalence, and hear it even without external support or encouragement. What I find affirming is embracing that God created me specifically with this Why prior to my being born. This comforts and strengthens me tremendously.

One way to hear this voice is to sit in silence for as long as you can. It might be uncomfortable, but that shouldn't stop you. You've already done some uncomfortable—maybe even very difficult—work as you've filled in your timeline.

You've visited the you of past successes and the you that saw them lost. You've remembered yourself as a viable, fulfilled person and also one who took wrong turns or was forced to take detours. You may have to double back and blaze a new path to a time when you felt viable and fulfilled. It's time right now to be in the present tense with the real you who listens to your true Why. So, sit in silence, be present with yourself and for yourself, and now ask:

Why was I born? Why am I here right now—not 50 years ago or 50 years from now—why am I here right now?

Let this be an exercise that examines every day and every week. Give that still, small voice more and more attention. Welcome it, allow it to announce itself, and do whatever is required to embody it. Trust yourself. Be grateful to all thoughts and leadings you hear.

This, of course, takes practice. It takes trying, and remember, trying can be, well, trying.

I was trained as a classical pianist. From age five to eighteen, my parents compelled me to take piano lessons. At times I resented it and, as soon as I could, I gave it up.

Years passed. At 30 years old I found myself missing the ability to play the piano. I decided that when I became 50 I'd go back to taking lessons.

The years passed until one day I awoke and said it was time. A few months ago I signed up for lessons.

Although my technique is extremely rusty, my soul feels elated to be playing again. I know a part of my Why is connected to playing the piano.

Is it difficult? Yes. Is finding practice time difficult? Yes. But each day—if I just open the piano and hit one note—if that's all I do, it's better than a year ago when playing was just a desire. The experience builds upon itself; I am improving more and more each day.

Just as I do, practice and let your experience build on itself. Tune into your Why daily; you'll be amazed by the results. You'll see that realizing and actualizing your Why gets easier. Like anything else, the more you train, the easier it becomes. You'll also become more resilient and resistant to any onslaught of negativity, despair, or regression.

By doing this exercise, you're giving yourself an opportunity to support and be true to what makes you feel one with whom you truly are.

It's about learning to cherish the feeling and knowing that feeling is a fabulous thing.

When you practice being one with whom you really are, you're learning to express who you really are, too. The voice of your Why is your voice, and using that voice feels great. You are walking in the certainty of whom you truly are.

> Adam was very athletic. His parents encouraged him to become a gymnast; it looked as if he'd make a fabulous one. He had the moves, he had the discipline, he had the commitment— but it wasn't his Why. His Why was ballet. Gymnastics might be parallel in its discipline, structure, and form, but the pursuit of it was not a fulfillment of his Why.
>
> In an effort to please his parents, Adam pursued gymnastics despite his true Why. How

could he lean toward ballet with his support system only endorsing gymnastics? How could he verbalize the voice that disagreed with his parents' wishes? He pursued gymnastics for a while and then stopped after a seemingly significant injury.

When Adam went off to college, he saw a request for persons interested in taking ballet lessons. He enrolled, trained, and discovered he loved it, and he ended up doing road shows for a major company in Europe.

For Adam, college wasn't the time he adopted someone else's Why, it was the time when he embraced and actualized his own. Drawn to ballet by the voice within him, the voice he could never tune out, the voice that resonated with his GPS.

LOOKING FORWARD TO USING YOUR GPS

Finding your Why actualizes your GPS. Yes, your God-prescribed perfect script! Once you know it, you can see the space narrowing between where you are and where you'd be if you were living it. This gives you a starting point.

Now that you have embraced your Why voice, you are in accord with your creator. You can pursue your Why together. As your connection to your Why continues to mature, you'll feel a confirmation of your path. You'll feel content and authentic, even pure. With Him, you will know you are on the right path.

When you do your daily practice of clocking in with your GPS, you'll basically get a confirmation to "continue on the straight path before you." This can be an important check-in.

Take time to speak with your God; ask Him to strengthen you as you move forward in fleshing out what it is that He had in mind when He created you for just this time and place. Continue to give the process of discovering your Why a nonjudgmental, affirming ear and, as you do so, bask in the total body experience.

Think about what it feels like, what it tastes like, what it sounds like. Embrace these moments of your life lived in peace with your Why. Go through all of your senses as a checklist. Let them instruct you. Should you continue straight or are you off course? Sensory information will provide the answers. Trust God to know the right course for you to take. In so doing delays, setbacks, pauses aren't then viewed as catastrophic but rather par for the course.

As mentioned before, spend time checking in with your maker. He knows with certainty why you were created. Not only can you dialog and assure yourself that you are on the right path, but God's perspective is a gift of reassurance itself. Good things, bad things, seeming ambiguities—they're all part of the plan, part of how the expression of your Why is distinct from anyone else's.

Drawing on God's support will keep you stalwart in pursuing a newly recognized purpose. Even if your support system actually endorses your Why, that endorsement may not be hearty enough—not to the degree that will bolster you while you create, continue, and sustain the changes that may occur in your life during this process. Only God can give you that unconditional support. After all, you are bringing forth His plan for your life.

Expect it—your Why will get tested at such times. When the trials descend you must arm yourself to face them by thinking about your Why and asking, *how badly do I want to know and live in my Why?*

Facing challenges to your Why helps it solidify you, which enables you to become stronger and more confident each time these challenges arise. Faced with these challenges you will become stronger and gather certainty and determination, coalescing a vision of a future where you live out your Why. These moments will hold you true and firmly to your path.

That vision of your future is a sight of compelling beauty and grace.

Successfully resisting the forces that might want to reclaim you from your true Why builds confidence. With that growing confidence, inspiration surges. More and more aspects of your being become aligned. Clarity follows, improving your vision.

You become willing: willing to spend the necessary time meditating and envisioning, willing to let yourself become bolstered by the Creator, willing to begin relying on the lucidity and certainty that comes with that relationship. You will see and appreciate how everything brought you to where you are right now, and it is a place of promise.

The Why, you suddenly find, is more than motivation, more than will—it is a guiding light and empowering force.

It is your deliverance! No wonder those who follow their Why feel lighter and more audacious!

Sound good? Of course it does! You've worked hard looking back. You can see now that the timeline of your life is a trail you've been following all along, destination after destination. You may have encountered your Why in the past or you may have decided what your Why definitely wasn't.

But now that you are practicing listening for and hearing the voice of your Why, you know that you don't have to wander along an unfulfilled trail of your life. You can instead move purposefully, intent on following the call of your Why, charting your course according to and along with that deepest core, that God-created being, which is your truest self. Committing to that provides a full understanding and embrace of your Why.

3
WHY WAS I CREATED?

Why was I created?

Asking implies that you accept you were created for a specific reason and that you don't feel you are currently fulfilling it to its entirety. I'll go further and say that you are a masterpiece in form and function:

Everything about you contributes to fulfilling the reason you are here.

In the most general sense, you were created to be human. Zeroing in, you were meant to walk, to talk, to dream, to think, to feel, as we all do. Zooming in further, you were created to walk your walk, dream your dreams, feel your feelings, express yourself as you need. In fact, you cannot help but be what you were created to be. You were created specifically for such a time as this.

Who are you?

It is in the answering of that question that you will find your Why. In that *who,* you'll find your Why. You were created to be you. You were created to fulfill you. So again, who are you? Answering that will take some inventorying because none of us can be summed up in one handy label.

We don't sum up objects that are important to us in a simple manner so how could we do that with ourselves? For instance, look at this example: When you go car-shopping, you might start off thinking, *I just need a car.* But "car" quickly becomes more nuanced and richer. The few must-have features you may have in mind are joined by those you never even hoped for. The more you shop, the sharper and clearer your desires become since you increase your exposure to all the possibilities available.

By the time you buy the car, it's not just any car, it's your car, customized according to your specifications. It possesses a specific make, model and color, a price-tag, mileage, a fuel efficiency rating; maybe it has a moon roof, automatic parallel parking features, leather seats—the car has transformed from a two-dimensional generic idea to a three-dimensional thing with a particular look and feel, not to mention possibly a new-car smell.

If someone asked you to describe this new car, you probably wouldn't leave it at being just a four-wheeled item with a cover and doors. Those adjectives would not be enough to capture its magnificent features, nor would they convey how the car made your car-driving experience better, more comfortable and distinctive.

In the same way, answering the question "Who am I?' points to your purpose, you've got to take notice of your features and how they function and manifest. To answer this question fully let us look at all kinds of factors for clues, from the obvious to the obscure, such as:

> What do my passions say about me?
> What does where I live say about who I am?
> Where would I like to live?
> What does what I like to watch and listen to mean?
> Why was I born in New York and not Australia, for instance?
> How does my being born there play a significant role in my Why?
> How did my position in my family or origin affect my Why?
> How does the fact that I failed at something impact my Why? Did I learn something or unlearn something that could be important?
> Having been abused, shot, divorced, or orphaned—any number of things—how does any of that impact my Why?

Some part of you might get impatient taking this inventory, complaining that what is being referenced has no bearing, but that's not so. Preferences, talents, everything that has happened to you whether of your own free will or not—they all play a part in your Why, even if they seem unrelated to some "Grand Plan." Remember that a GPS—a Global Positioning System—no matter your detours, will continue to direct you and re-direct you to your desired and programmed destination.

It's the same with our human GPS. It's your life path. Each aspect of it—every feature, its terrain, your experiences, your lessons—all of it is your journey. All of it is relevant, and it's all significant to the fulfillment of your created purpose. These pieces are the moving parts to your evolving Why, in real time as only you can live it. Who are you? All of its parts signify Why you were created. Why were you created? Accepting this will help you find the propelling force behind it all so that you can sail this vessel called you through the tides of life, using the winds instead of fighting against them.

THE DETOUR THAT SHOWED ME THE WAY OF MY WHY

I've already mentioned that I was a preacher's daughter. I was born into an environment rich with religious faith, practice, philosophy, and values. Unfortunately, there was a time in my life when I rebelled against my upbringing and rejected it all.

Away from what was true for me, my core self grew restless. I did things I thought would fill me, but they didn't work. As a friend of mine put it, I was like a corpse on the dance floor, going through the motions, doing the steps, trying to fit in, but stinking at it the entire time.

As I began my own self-examination, it became clear that a significant part of my Why includes my spiritual roots as a person who had to find a life path that celebrates her creator, appreciating all that He provides. My Why could only thrive and be encouraged by a well-grounded, nurturing, spiritual way of life. Without this in my life, I realized that I was not the leader-servant I was created to be. My family's religious affiliation—namely the Religious Society of Friends, Quakers, was significant to my Why.

Without total acceptance of these spiritual and religious factors in my life, I was only attempting to be something I wasn't. I wasn't living true to my Why and created purpose and I didn't ring true to myself. Seeing me from the outside, people around me might have thought I fit in and was doing okay, but that wasn't the case. The problem was that the very fabric of my being and my soul felt empty. My knowledge of Janet felt empty, negative, and without focus. I was lost from my core. I was lost in my core.

That changed when I began asking the why questions I have asked you to ask of yourself: *why was I created?*

I made my discoveries and then embraced the fact that God created me for a purpose. That purpose included all the facets of my family of origin. That heritage was the foundation God expected me to build upon in order to discover my created purpose—not abandon. When I took ownership of the spiritual pieces of my Why, I got clarity and certainty back and began to feel whole. I had to own it all in order to own me. That release and peace of mind was essential.

TAKE OWNERSHIP

This process of self-reflection, the lessons gleaned from your timeline, the stock you take of the here and now along with your daily silence exercise —they have given your Why an audience and helped you hear its voice more clearly. What has it been telling you? What do you now know about your Why? It's important to embrace the thoughts that have arisen.

> *You'll notice, going forward, that the more you accept why you were created, the more able you'll be to see confirmations of this knowledge throughout different facets and events in your life.*

Stack those confirmations and test them. See what rings true for you.

Consider this, for example: When I call myself by my given name Janet, do I really know that's who I am? What if I called myself another name, say, Elizabeth? It wouldn't work, would it? It wouldn't ring true to what I have known to be me. I may know an Elizabeth, but she isn't me.

When I say Janet, on the other hand, I feel a sense of ownership, a sense of understanding, a sense of knowing every aspect of Janet—where Janet's toe begins, where Janet's fingers begin, Janet's nose, Janet's elbow, Janet's knees—my name becomes a whole-body experience. I own it. Janet is me. I can hug, kiss, compliment, and encourage Janet and feel an immediate reaction without ever opening my mouth.

I am unique.

I differ from everyone, even from someone else whose name is Janet, whose middle initial is M, who was born in the same hospital, around the same time, delivered by the same doctor—that other Janet still differs from me and so does her created purpose.

Her footprint differs from mine. Even identical twins have different sets of fingerprints. Our fingerprints are external indicators of our differences, but we have internal markers, too, which also point to uniqueness. This goes all the way down to our souls. There, too, is a unique printing. This unique printing was created by God as my Perfect Script—

my Human GPS. It is the blueprint to the fulfillment of my Why. It is my purpose in this world.

REJECTING YOUR PURPOSE

What a beautiful world it would be if everyone really took the time to understand their unique contribution to the world. Many people, unfortunately, reject the idea of doing that. They don't want the responsibility of truly owning themselves and evolving into a person who purposely and purposefully seeks to find and live out a unique mission. They might reject that path to avoid standing out. They might not want to take the time or do the necessary work to get there. Perhaps they tried and when it got difficult, they quit.

Rejecting the path, these souls just remain in place or else trudge along the repetitive circles of their days until the next time the question of "Why?" insists on being heard. That's not living at all, is it?

They are, as I was long ago, corpses at a dance.

Living in such a way puts you in survival mode when God meant you to thrive and enjoy life. You've got to be true to who you were created to be even if you feel like there isn't something unique about you beyond your fingerprints.

Maybe you see the similarities between you and others and think you're just ordinary. Yes, perhaps your path does parallel the paths of others, but think about that: Parallel lines never merge. Even if you are doing similar things in close proximity to another, your paths are your own and your individualized purposes are just that.

I've asked you to embrace your differences, those things that make you unique. I want you to embrace your similarities to others, as well. Perhaps by being in such close proximity and walking parallel paths, you are someone who can truly understand what another is facing. You support and encourage those close to you.

You can also receive their support and learn supportive techniques from them that you can apply to yourself. Perhaps they will learn from you. In our similarities lies the ability to relate to our fellow travelers. Fingerprints, while different, are also very similar; they tag us as fellow humans. The same can be said about your purpose. It can be in a well-populated area where friends await.

Purpose doesn't have to be grand; it doesn't have to reside in uncharted territory.

It can have similarities to another's purpose while still possessing its own element of uniqueness.

So, don't question it. Don't judge it. Don't decide it has to look a certain way for it to be legitimate. If you question your Why instead of answering its call, you could end up like so many unfortunate others, rejecting your purpose and never discovering what it really is. Your Why is a permanent part of you, lurking within you whether you give it voice or not, whether you answer it or not.

Not everyone is open to it, confident enough to entertain it and brave enough to face it; doing so challenges and rattles what you've been doing with yourself so far. Face it or not, the question recurs: Why were you created?

Some people are lucky enough to discover their purpose early in life; others take longer. The good news—and, for the more resistant among you, the bad news is—that far, far into the future, you'll still find your Why waiting for you along your path. You can either recognize it as your guide right now, or wait for it to be your regret when you look back and realize the scope of your deprivation, not only the deprivation inflicted on yourself but on the world. Any time you feel stuck, unfulfilled, frustrated, or confronted with adversity, the question of your purpose may come up.

Act now!

Yes, for some of you, following your Why might take time and energy, rake up difficult issues, and at times seem overwhelming. But giving in to the notion that discovering your Why and examining it costs too much robs the world of your gift. And it robs you.

Is that truly what you want?

THE ANOMALIES

I've discussed this with some who say there is no such thing as a GPS (God's Perfect Script). Not everyone has a Why, they say, and yet those folks still go places. Do you belong to that school of thought? Have you ever known someone who is both successful and fulfilled who isn't living from a place of inspired passion? Successful, fulfilled people who are living from a place of inspired passion are living in their Why.

Your Why asks you to be inspired. It asks you to be authentic. Living according to your Human GPS enables you to live a life full of inspiration. It means you show up whole and complete, ungoverned by external things. When you live your Why, you have everything you need to live true and truly live.

Remember, your support system, family, friends, education—all things in your environment are external. It's not that they have no role or importance. External forces may validate you, help keep you on the straight and narrow, empower you as you go along your journey. But a welcomed, owned Why, as well as an understood purpose is what enables you to continue the journey to living your created truth.

That is glorious.

4

ADJUSTING YOUR PERSPECTIVE AS YOU JOURNEY THROUGH LIFE

I haven't emphasized enough, so far, the need to talk regularly with your creator about what He had in mind when He created you. As you do so, realize you live your Why in a progression, challenged in different ways at various junctures of your life. These are times when you will need to stay connected to Him, waiting, listening, talking, and even sometimes crying and screaming out to Him.

There will come a time or times when you must encourage yourself as you go forward, knowing that He is with you and will never leave you alone. After all, He created you with this purpose even for such a time as this. He is the only one who knows what awaits you beyond the horizon; your road may bring experiences that defy expectation.

The fact that He is your creator means He knows your beginning and your end. He knows the reason for everything that has and hasn't happened in your life. Nothing catches Him by surprise. He has specifically allowed it all for a reason. Even with those very ugly things in life, when you trust Him, you will see the benefit down the road along your journey.

Once you actually arrive at your destination, it may look different from what you imagined. It might, to your surprise, be the starting point for another journey that has a better destination. Don't be dismayed.

Your Why is your reason for being; all situations, as previously stated, are created specifically for you and will be throughout your life.

Is it really a surprise that life will always have need of you being truly you, truly alive, resisting stagnation in favor of bearing fruit? Your seasons are many and your Why will bring many harvests. Trust God. He has a plan.

Your interests may change as you get older. This, too, may cause you some worry. Trusting God is a treasure, buried within it is joy in times of worry and anxiety. When you regularly check in with your creator and are in an aligned relationship with Him, you can be at peace with what He points to as His desire for you. So, yes: You will have to update or hone your Why as you age, just as you have to update your manmade navigational GPS system. Rest assured, though, that as long as you are alive, your creator has the complete view of your life. He knows where you're headed. As you grow older, your environment may change. You may feel different physically, but the fact that you have a purpose won't change even at your tender age.

The secret is that we are more like vines than stones. This life is about your journey, not about your destination.

Embrace the fact that yours is an eternal journey. There is pleasure in that, but also trepidation. Don't let the trepidation stop you—that's what keeps so many people from fully uncovering their Why. Of course, there's comfort in predictability and also comfort in knowing exactly what you're going to do without having to question or explore. But that comfort will never bring the complete joy that comes when you know that every cell in your body, every fiber of your being is joined together and working in one accord, all fulfilling your Why, regardless of the troubles that befall you along the way.

Take me and my piano lessons as an example. I don't know where, at fifty-nine years old, my current piano lesson pursuit will take me. But at twenty, thirty, forty, and in my early fifties, I knew it was something I wanted to revisit. Though I don't necessarily know the destination of this venture, I do know that my Why is involved in it. Is this pursuit for my own pleasure? Is this to bring enjoyment to my family and friends when they visit? Is this going to be an integral part of my coaching? I don't know. I don't need to know.

What I do know and all I need to know is that these lessons are a part of my created purpose, which is to lead and serve. Knowing that is enough for me. I am growing, enjoying this season of my life as my Why bears its fruits in its own time—in God's own time. It is difficult at this age to find time to practice; it is taking longer to learn than it did when I was in my teens. At times it is very frustrating, it is at those times that I walk away from the process for a few hours and enjoy things that give me pleasure, like swimming, hiking, and listening to what nature has to tell me. Because piano playing is a part of my created purpose, I return to it after the break, feeling whole, renewed, and complete, ready to tackle that which was previously frustrating.

FIND DIRECTION IN FINDING YOUR DIRECTION

Even with clarity about where you want to go, you'll still have to fight through your own skepticism. Remember, you are not the originator of your life. As I previously noted, knowing you can trust your creator is a comfort and source of strength. In moments of ambiguity, trepidation, or uncertainty, being in a peaceful and accepting relationship with the truth that you were created for a purpose will fuel you to continue the journey. Not only does being centered on God's guidance center you internally, it keeps you aligned in any environment and supports you. Without this, your journey will be infinitely more difficult.

David was raised in a Christian home. As he got older, he grew estranged from God and all religious practice. Now in his mid-fifties and a grandparent, life for him had been, in his own words, good. As he saw his parents age, he began reflecting on their life and wondering what he will be like at their age.

Sharing his reflections with me, he confided that there had always been a part of him that felt something was missing. He said that despite doing well financially, professionally, socially, and as a spouse and father, he has always wondered if he was living the life he was created to live. I gave him an assignment to research bible verses that describe a longing for God.

When he returned after doing that, he told me he'd felt as if there was a tune within him that was missing its verse; reading those bible passages, he'd found the missing words to his song. Beginning in his early twenties, he said, he'd been feeling not fully engaged in life. As he'd initially stated, that was the time when he began to walk away from God and the religious practices he had grown up with.

As our sessions progressed, the onion, as it were, unpeeled: Despite his seeming success, the core of his being was unfulfilled. I mentioned the GPS analogy to him. Yes, he answered, it was as if he had turned off the GPS navigation system in his life at twenty. Now he wonders what events in his life would have been similar and what would have been different had he not turned it off. He wanted now to explore his Why so that when he gets to the age of his parents, he can feel assured, knowing he has had fulfilled his life's purpose.

David re-dedicated his life to Christ and now works on a volunteer basis with young people in their freshman year of college. He encourages them to bring Christ with them to school. By sharing his experiences, David is making a significant impact in the lives of students who for the first time might be away from home, parents, and childhood practices and norms.

To stimulate the type of change just described, many people don't care to ask those questions of themselves. Their lives have perhaps been easy, comfortable, successful, or all three. They've grown accustomed to that state of affairs, society views them as successful, and that may bolster a sense that questioning isn't really necessary. Many of those same people if they're honest within themselves, admit to an unresolved feeling that something has been—is—missing, and they have yearned for more.

*A **widespread rationalization** says life is never easy, which can sometimes lull you into a place of complacency, even comfort against internal disquiet.*

This false sense of comfort often suppresses the yearning to answer the question, am I being all I was created to be. Many uphold the belief that it is okay to go to the grave having never found an answer to our questions or a resolution to the feelings that keep welling up from that longing for a purpose fulfilled. Why should we accept that? Why would we? Why would we accept that as we draw our last breath, we do so as incomplete versions of ourselves who let the most fertile parts of our being lay fallow?

Discover your Why. You owe it to the world. When you decide not to explore your potential, you deprive the world of your service. The fallow parts of your being need sowing and feeding. Right now, nestled within are bits of yourself that you're ignoring. The grave comes soon enough. Stop denying bits of yourself. Seize your Why to seize your life so that your last breath isn't a sigh of resignation, but one of peaceful satisfaction.

What does your current belief system say about that? Does it tell you that questioning is a distraction from your "real life"?—a tiresome interruption brought on by adverse circumstances that will pass like a bout of indigestion? Does it perhaps even tell you that questioning is dangerous? Do your beliefs about life try to convince you that despite your and every other human's uniqueness, we are all just somehow supposed to lead cookie cutter lives? Do your life beliefs take your purpose into account at all?

Just to reconfirm. I believe that all things work together for my good. God created me. He knew me before anyone else did. He knows me better than I know myself. He had something specific in mind when He created me, and I believe I must actualize that purpose. It is also my firm belief that the good, the bad, and the ugly have a place in my created purpose, and although it is oft-times very painful, I trust and believe in His plan for my life.

Because I stand firm on this belief, I give Him my life, allowing Him to transform and govern it. I trust Him because He knows me best. He has a plan for my life. God knows exactly how my life will turn out, so I trust Him and the perfect script He has written for my life.

My trust and certainty are a result of the history of our established relationship. If you have a pet, it trusts you to be dependable, loving, caring, and forgiving. The same happens with our children. They trust that as their parents, we know what's going on. If anything goes awry, a child enjoys a sense of certainty: "My daddy is going to fix it. My momma is going to help me. I don't have to worry." The history of events up until that point gives the child the assurance that Mom and Dad are reliable and have the child's best interest at heart.

For those of you who are not parents, think of something you own or have created. If you have a favored recipe, for instance, you trust it because of the number of times you have created and enjoyed it. You are certain you can count on that recipe; it will perform for you. It is tried and tested.

God created you. He counts on you to become what He made you to be, and you can count on Him to make sure you turn out as planned. If we approach life from that standpoint, then we know with confidence what is true for us even if everyone else is heading in a different direction. When we face obstacles, we can live in that safe place of certainty. We know where we are going, where we need to be, and who we are because we are relying not on our own ability, but on the plan of our creator.

WHEN OUR ENVIRONMENT CHANGES

Paul has pastored his entire life. That's all he's known, and even though he's in his late eighties he still hasn't retired! His wife tells him he should, but pastoring is the thing that has fulfilled his Why. He wonders: If he stops doing it now, how will he fulfill his Why? Part of our coaching experience was to examine his "call to ministry." What does standing in the pulpit do for him? What does it authenticate within him?

During our sessions, he was able to express his fear, which was that his purpose wouldn't age with him. Happily, after a few sessions, we were able to clarify how his call to teach and lead could definitely be fulfilled in retirement. He had a moving realization: He would always be a teacher, whether or not it's from a pulpit.

Paul then realized that his peers could use his teaching, support, and guidance. Paul began to mentor other pastors, which led to his writing several books. He began to hold seminars for pastors in their mid-fifties and older on how to transition from the pulpit while still being used by God. He became a support system for other octogenarians. These mentored pastors have fulfilled their careers; many of them have been retired longer than they'd ever worked, and they wondered what their purpose could be. Having seen Paul redefine his created purpose they too have the hope and courage to follow suit.

During his seminars, Paul highlighted the need for octogenarians to explore and embrace a post-retirement purpose of embodying a living legacy. There was peace in that for him. It's better than being disgruntled but continuing to preach as he had known for fear of what he could and would do if he retired.

He chose peace versus living out a curmudgeonly attitude! Our purpose, as Paul demonstrates, can take different forms and expressions as we age, but remain fulfilling, nonetheless.

CHANGING YOUR LENS DOESN'T HAVE TO BE A SOLO MISSION

Trusting God's Perfect Script enables us to live with the confidence that we can shift from human power to God's power with the assurance that He has created us for such a time as that in which we find ourselves. This is a significant shift in perspective, changes how we view everything.

If you feel unsure about how to start embracing this perspective on your own, it's time to get a coach.

With a coach, even if you feel clueless or lost about where to begin, you can develop awareness and learn the techniques you need to discover your own Why.

The process may be unfamiliar, it might even be uncomfortable in the beginning, but with consistent coaching, you'll be able to move to that place of certainty and fulfillment within.

A coach will help you work through the questions I've posed so far and others to come. It will be a judgement-free relationship; through it will come affirmation and a growing awareness that you're doing the best you can. Your coaching relationship can transform your life, help you reveal your Why, and ready you to start living it.

5

FROM POINT A TO POINT B

You've probably gathered by now that for me faith and belief in a power larger than yourself are essential to purpose. Someone is responsible for creating you at such a time as this, and because of that there is a reason for your being created at this point in time.

I understand some readers will be skeptical of this. Remember, though, that even in Darwinism there is a beginning. There is always a starting point. Even if you're not entirely sure where, how, or who, I encourage you to open your heart to the truth that you were started intentionally.

There is a reason why you're here, and you've been given a uniqueness that is yours alone to wield in this world. Without a specialized purpose, God would not have gone to such an effort to ensure that each of us is so special and unique, even down to our fingerprints.

You are a masterpiece with a significant part to play in this world. As an exceptional being, you were created to live into your true identity. Just one hair from your head can identify you—that's how important your identity is, and you must live it— your purpose—out.

No matter the circumstances under which you came into the world, the minute you clocked in, your identity and purpose were entered into eternity. Regardless of your philosophical belief, your existence means that you are here to live out a purpose meant for you alone. Our legacy lives on after we die: Martin Luther King, Mother Teresa, Gandhi, Ben Franklin—all contributed something so unique that they still affect our lives today. Their souls' fingerprints live on. Even a baby that dies at birth influences the world of those who knew and interacted with the infant, creating a ripple effect that spreads through history.

Did you know that there are documented cases where an organ transplant recipient's personality has shifted, even their likes and dislikes? For example, an older person who received a younger person's heart began enjoying a different music genre. There are even cases where an organ recipient was able to mysteriously provide evidence against the killer of that organ's donor. (For more information about these phenomena, see "Change of Heart" by Claire Sylvia.) For the donors, traces of their lives continue on.

It also shows that, though we always supposed the brain to be the center of all our personal knowledge, there is cellular communication and cellular memory in other parts of our body—our identities live on to the very cell. To me, it makes complete sense that there's a creator behind such exceptional powerful identities as ours.

This is why for me, if exceptional is possible, mediocrity is unacceptable. Admittedly, this notion for some can be as terrifying as it is wonderful.

If you want to go from believing you have a Why to finding it and now finally living it—if you want to move from your beginning through to your ending fulfilled, then you're best served by relying on the Alpha and the Omega, namely God. He knows your Why, He knows how to help you discover it, He knows where your needed resources are, He knows the best routes. It's time to flip on the GPS and follow God's Perfect Script!

EN ROUTE

At this point, you should have, after a lot of reflection and listening for God's guidance, figured out your

Why. Are you born to serve, born to lead, born to create? Whatever you've discovered, you will have grounded yourself in it. Hopefully, you've even figured out where you need to go next.

So how do you actually go from here to there? How do you tie these two ideas—knowing your Why and knowing where you need to go—how do you tie them together?

The process is not unlike that of personal training: it's tough stuff. This isn't going to be an easy road. An integral part of your success will be building and solidifying your foundation. Just like your first few weeks or months with a personal trainer, you will discover areas of discomfort that you were previously unaware of.

Strength gets built upon a solid foundation. It's layer upon layer upon layer of change. Each level is filled with obstacles you have overcome, and they then become embedded and solidified as you move from level to level. The first driver on an unpaved road is going to face extreme bumpiness, but after a while the path becomes smooth and easier to drive on over time. More and more clarity comes as you move forward and you hone in on more and more things that confirm your created purpose.

Even if your Why is extremely broad early on, as you work through it, your GPS will become clearer and your destination more certain. Just as with a global positioning system, the closer you get to the programmed destination, the more confirmations the system gives you.

The first step is to make an action plan. A corporate entity will make monthly, and then quarterly goals. The calendar year gets broken up into bite-sized chunks. Similarly, with individuals, we break down our timeframe into manageable segments.

As you gather successes, you build on them until you achieve your goal. Very often what initially evolves is bigger than you can envision. If your goal, let's say, is to lose 20 pounds, start by focusing on that first half pound. What would it take on a daily basis to lose just that?

As an overview, it will be a lot easier to answer questions if you can assess where you are right now. What are the factors that are contributing to your status quo? Get a full understanding of your own situation by answering this question honestly.

Maybe you're a fancy coffee enthusiast but know those coffees and midday croissants are a serious source of empty calories. Don't just blindly try and quit cold turkey. Instead investigate: Ask yourself, Why do you so regularly choose that midday snack? Are there social reasons contributing to it? In a big city, everyone is so on-the-go. Stopping at the coffee shop where everyone goes can help you feel like you belong. If you force yourself to give that up cold turkey, your diet is going to be harder. In this example, if the social experience fuels your snacking, consider continuing to go to your favorite coffee shop, but just change the snacks you buy.

Maybe going to this particular coffee shop makes you feel that you have attained a certain degree of financial status. Is it about the pride that comes from knowing you're able to afford coffee from this place? Maybe when you were less financially able, you went to the cheaper competitor.

Now in your mind you've so progressed in your career and financial status that you no longer need to settle with the corner store coffee and pastry. If that's the case, do you really need to spend ten dollars to ingest 700 calories? Or can you enjoy the environment at this new coffee shop, enjoy the fellowship, but also enjoy a coffee that is less calories or even zero calories? These are the things you need to look at.

It's not about motivation; it's about inspiration, which comes from within.

What energizes you now are the things and behaviors that fulfill your purpose. Those behaviors, and your approach to your life and the events therein—these control your outcome.

CORPORATE STRATEGIES

Corporately, the same strategy to pursuing Why applies. Let's say you want to move from making

$500,000 a year in revenue to $900,000 or even millions. What does that mean? Does it mean that you go out and hire ten more people? Does it mean that you hire three more people? Does it mean getting 20 more clients?

To begin with, you've got to look at who your staff members are right now. What are their strengths? Are they operating in their Why? If so, it might be more a matter of adjusting the corporate setting than hiring new people.

Company B thought that as they grew, they needed to hire someone to their team. Instead, when they looked within and understood the Whys of their current team, they realized that all the company needed to do was switch around some job functions, relying on people's strengths and passions. Everyone was happier working in their respective Whys. The company effectively accommodated the teams and grew to a very productive company!

When people are working into and within their Why, phenomenal ideas come up. This team was able to discover ways in which they, without adding any work hours and without changing anything except a focus on their Whys, attracted more business.

The company never had to change their expenditures or hire anyone else. With committed and dedicated people working from their Whys, business soared. Their corporation grew significantly and now they have several branches around the world.

How? I was able to assess that during business hours team members were obsessed with their cellphones.

When I presented this to them during initial sessions, they responded that they desired to remain connected and didn't want to miss anything on social media. Instead of seeing that as an annoyance, I asked a very simple question: *How could we use that desire to contribute to your work and help the company?*

Employees began doing social media postings for the company, improving the company's marketing aspects, and created a gaming program that enabled a previously seasonal business to become a year-round entity. They also used drones to personalize the business, providing customers with real-time before, during, and after images.

Interestingly enough, personal cellphone time diminished significantly and production increased. The company was able to bring a dimension never before provided to the profession.

When an integration of personal and corporate Whys got merged serious innovations and possibilities opened up.

Let me add that this company never had a mission statement. I allowed each employee to state their strengths and their Why and thereby everyone felt more invested in the company's success. They could own the success and progress of the company as their own success and progress because their Whys and created purpose had contributed to corporate success and growth.

IT'S TIME BECAUSE YOU ARE ALREADY WHOLE

There is a misunderstanding that might have come from reading thus far. Perhaps you're assuming, even subconsciously, that you have to be relatively healthy, well balanced, successful, and devoid of any disability to live into you Why. As our corporate friends discovered, that is simply not true.

Remember that when they called me in, they were not thriving. In fact, they were on the verge of filing bankruptcy. Together we looked at what was going on in real time re-oriented their viewpoints and they were able in the end to glean corporate and individual success. You're enough right now. Take my brother, for instance: People like him, born with a developmental disability, can still live into their Why. Greatness is just as much theirs as anyone else's.

Another example: There is a writer and television director named Simon Fitzmaurice who, because of ALS, has lost the ability to speak and write. He can only communicate with his eyes—he writes by pointing his eyes. He uses a Tobii I-15 eye-gaze computer to communicate. Some might say he should accept his disability and live out his days. But instead, Simon was determined to live his Why and allowed nothing to prevent him from living out his created purpose.

You're never dysfunctional enough, you're never disabled enough, you're never impoverished enough, you're never wealthy enough—there is no excuse for you not living your created purpose or Why.

Levels, be they medically, psychologically, or economically, do not serve as an excuse for ignoring or not fulfilling your purpose.

Wherever you are, whatever your circumstances, you can live into your Why. As long as you are alive, there is a purpose and a reason Why you're still here. Get a coach, together discover your created purpose, and start down the path of your Why. Time is passing and you are depriving the world of the reason you are here.

6
GETTING BACK ON TRACK

Even when you've got a GPS, even if you've pinpointed your location, your destination, and your route—even with all the preparation you can muster—there will still be unintentional detours. You may, for instance, miss a turn. How do we respond to these hurdles?

A crucial thing to remember is that life allows us to pull over. We must all take this time for reflection. In my belief system, my creator God rested on the seventh day and reflected on what He had done. You must follow that example to reflect, reorient, and refuel. Give yourself space to recalibrate. Within the days and nights between your life's beginning and your end you'll take many such rest stops. Reversals and disruptions, they are not just necessary, but essential.

No matter your goal, issues will arise that affect your progress. Environmental, emotional, and/or physical matters will create extenuating circumstances that interfere with or move you off your route altogether. But God knew about all this long before you were born. Your GPS is still working. Learn to embrace the obstacles rather than condemn or fight them. Those are circumstantial, unlike your GPS (God's Perfect Script), which is permanent. Embrace the flow, reflect, on what you can learn and gain from it. You will build on those moments as you move forward. They will be the footpath upon which the enriched experiences of your future will be built.

HOW TO TELL WHEN YOU'VE SWERVED OFF COURSE

If you feel out of sorts and it's not a passing mood, something is off. Doubt, fear, frustration, anxiety, condemnation—they are all red flags that you've possibly swerved off course.

What you're experiencing doesn't have to be negative. Departures from the natural pace of things may be signs of an inadvertent detour. No one can go 100 miles an hour forever. No one can stay still forever either. Yes, there may be times when there's intense speed and action, but that's always going to be followed by the balance of rest. If there's no balance, beware.

*The understanding and embrace of your flow
promote longevity.*

When you recognize those signs, stop, reflect, investigate, and reorient. Can you recognize where you are and how you got there? Understanding what contributed to a possible detour will be invaluable in getting back on track and facilitate your awareness of where you are.

Sometimes you're not off course but traveling through an intersection where it's possible to miss your turn if you're not alert. For instance, if you're running what just became a mid-cap corporation and you got there at warp speed, what's the next proper step? Aim to be the top of line? Soar ahead? Or just live where you are at for now, embrace the new situation, to really reap the benefits of the changes the company has enjoyed?

It may be tempting to soar ahead, but that may not be in your best interest. Pushing forward may be a plan for next quarter, next year, or five years from now. Remember this is about the journey. The journey unfolds over time.

HITTING THE BRAKES

When I returned to New York ten years ago to care-give my parents and brother, I did so without my husband. Although married, in New York I had the ability to create a schedule and routine that satisfied my needs. I had a well-paved groove in place. I exercised when I wanted for as long as I wanted, I ate when I wanted, I cooked or didn't cook as I desired, and I had a variety of routines and interests that choreographed nicely with my caregiving and NYC lifestyle. My routine was very health conscious. My parents also embraced that lifestyle, so all of my environments were supportive of my Why.

Things changed when I left New York and went back to Texas after my parents and brother transitioned to their final resting place. The adjustments were many. I returned to being a full-time wife, Mom, Grandma, and Great-Grandma again. My schedule had to accommodate a few more people, social demands, and obligations. Life took on a much different look than I had known for the past 10 years.

In addition to all those adjustments, I was no longer in my 50s, and there were some physical and medical changes that manifested four months after I moved back to Texas. The ability to walk to destinations as I did in NYC was not possible. My schedules were irregular, workouts became less formalized, inconsistent at best, and my body was changing in several ways.

Texas is known as the obesity capital of the United States, so my environment was not supportive of my health and I was overwhelmed to say the least with the challenges all around. It became easier to just nestle in to the status quo, use the excuse of wanting to fit into my relationship and deny what my soul was crying out for.

I missed the supports of my old lifestyle. In New York, even if I didn't want to exercise, the gym window was to my left as I walked into my building and neighbors would wave hello encouragingly, continually reigniting the significance of a healthy lifestyle to my Why.

The Texas environment, on the other hand, endorsed eating with reckless abandon and was 100% sedentary. I began to gain weight. The holidays rolled around, and I was 15 pounds heavier than I had been just 10 months prior. I back-burnered my weight. My justification was I had been away for a long time and I didn't want to stand out any more than I had to. I began embodying a lifestyle that was not true to who I was or who I was created to be. I felt stuck and in trouble.

One day, when I really looked at myself in the mirror I asked, "Where are you going? What is this all about? Whose life are you living?"

The answer to those questions caused me to pump the brakes, sit, and address the answers to the questions asked.

It was time to reevaluate. Before my initial move to Texas 12 years earlier, I was told by my God that when I went to Texas, I must be the "salt" in my environment. Gaining the ten, fifteen, and then twenty pounds emotionally impeded my ability to be that salt because I was no longer living true to who I knew myself to be. I was pretending in order to fit in, which ultimately hurt me significantly. I was not living true to my created purpose.

ADAPTING TO NEW ENVIRONMENT

I had to re-orient and you might have to, as well. In my case, I needed to embrace my continued and redefined Why along with my changing environment, my age and medical issues, and my newly defined roles. I engaged a coach, and together we re-clarified a few things. My Why was still as true for me here in Texas as it had been in New York. We examined the emotions behind the need to fit in, as well as the emotions around the physical and medical challenges that all came following the loss of my family members and my relocation.

A renewed Why manifested. I was now being fine-tuned to revolutionize people's lives. Reviewing my journal entries facilitated my re-connective process. Time spent fellowshipping, praising, and thanking God for all He had blessed me with during my journaling time was revealing.

I sat in my backyard, listened to the birds, and thanked them for being true to who they were created to be. I thanked the butterflies for surviving their transformational process. I thanked the rain for providing nourishment and water to the needed plants, reservoirs, pools and other bodies of water. I thanked myself for being willing to reconnect with my created purpose despite the many challenges. I hugged myself, I kissed myself, I appreciated every seen and unseen part of my body for doing the things they do without my asking or telling. This was and continues to be a daily routine that would only have been integrated into my life as a result of seeming failures caused by my overarching desire to fit in and the resulting weight gain.

Living true to my Why as a 60-year-old whose body environment, outer environment, and social environment have changed, I look to the constant gifts in my life for anchoring. These constants for me are revealed through nature and the awesomeness of things in my life like breathing, moving, thinking—things so readily overlooked, taken for granted, and oft-times seen as insignificant.

These times spent with God, nature, and being appreciative reemphasized what being truly meant. I understood that at 60, the deposits I put into the lives of those I encounter must be well-seasoned and tasteful.

Out of the abundance of my life, my cries, my frustrations, setbacks, and disappointments will reveal an array of possibilities. Not solely through words but also through my deeds and seeming failures others will be significantly supported, guided, and encouraged to live their created purpose.

CONCLUSION

EVERYTHING MEANS SOMETHING

First thing this morning, there were two birds fighting on my deck. They were both so engrossed with their fight that they threw themselves against my glass door. It was shocking. It seemed like a fight for territory, and it held a lesson for me: Sometimes I, too, get so caught up in turmoil with a member of my own species that I end up hurting myself and others way more than it is worth.

I might think I'm going somewhere—those birds thought they were moving through open space—but instead I, like the birds, end up slamming into a wall literally or figuratively. How many times have I reacted in that manner instead of taking a quick breath, pausing, or just walking away? Any of those actions could have saved the day or prevented broken emotions and/or relationships.

When I saw the birds, I knew this didn't just happen; it was all created and timed for me to witness at that very time. I saw it for a reason. It was scripted for me to gain a deeper understanding into my Why, and because I was open to the lesson, I learned deeply from it. The larger lesson I gained from this experience did not come from the two fighting birds. There was another bird perched on the fence looking at all of this. After they both hit the glass door, that other bird came down and looked at them both chirped at them and flew away with the fighters.

The lesson for me was that as I live in my created purpose I am called at times to stand alone from a vantage point that sees things slightly differently. With that insight, I must come down to the levels of hurt and pain suffered by those like me, give my input and fly high alongside them into our determined future.

Everything, everything, everything means something.

The timing, the sequence, and experience of everything is significant. The rain or sun on your face, the laughter or cries you hear, the tastes of a sample at the store, the sight of two birds fighting—they all mean something and cannot be disregarded.

Everything has a part to play in your Why. Events in this very moment of your life are God's Perfect Script for the evolution, understanding, and clarification of your Why.

As the script of your life unfolds, embrace the understanding that everything provides a beautiful mosaic piece to the living out of your Why.

In some places in the world, bathroom sinks have one spigot for hot water and one for cold. The difficulty comes in trying to combine what comes out of them individually so that you can have warm water. In our own lives, there are times when collecting the extreme events of our lives and finding a way to blend them is challenging.

In the face of such occasions, there are at least two possibilities:

1. Ignore the situations by saying none pertain to you.
2. Select portions of the situation that feel most comforting.

The difficulty with either of these choices is that the risk is that there are significant cues and clues that bare relevance to your Why. Taking the time to regulate and balance the extreme experiences in life creates an environment within your being where you can flourish and live a life that is true to your purpose.

Appreciation is also an important key. When you adopt a lifestyle of appreciation and thankfulness for the times, places, and experiences given, you create opportunities where revelations and understanding flow. Life's experiences become clarifying moments that all yield to your living your created purpose.

ALWAYS EVOLVE

The most important thing to remember from this book is not just your Why, but the fact that your Why is not fixed. It's not as if as soon as you figure it out, you are good for life.

> *Your Why will change and evolve as you evolve. As your physiological, intellectual, financial, cognitive, and emotional environments change, your Why will adjust accordingly.*

As you move and grow through your days and seasons, different hungers will emerge. Anytime you're in a place of questioning, a time of wondering, *could there be more?* or, *what if?* —know that your Why is yearning for recognition. There is either a need for tweaking your Why or, if you have never been previously cognizant of your Why, there is a need to discover it. When you yearn for something, even if it is as simple as a new outfit or car, a piece of your Why is in that desire.

Cars and outfits won't fulfill you, as stated previously. True fulfillment has to be internally based because if it isn't there is no lasting power to it. Taking the car example, it is hoped that the acquisition of that new car will fulfill the yearning within, correct? So why does the desire so often dissipate faster than the new car smell does? Maybe because our external yearnings are simply beacons of light that orient to those matters internal. Using those emerging desires as you navigate, facilitates clarity and gained insight into you evolving Why.

LET IT CARRY YOU

You've known someone who sat in a chair only to have it break. Does that prevent you from sitting in chairs at all? No. It doesn't even concern you enough to investigate every chair before sitting down. Life goes on and you don't live it in fear of the stray exceptional event.

Even though your path may be punctuated by accidents or unpredictable traumas, it doesn't prevent you from living life. Your purpose is to live, to continue on. Wouldn't it be better if, along the way, especially in the face of difficulties, you could find deeper value?

That's where your Why comes in. It's the deepest, value of your life. It supports and empowers you.

When my clients are having a hard time accepting events in their life, I often ask if they are able to swim. If so, I ask them to find a pool, walk into a depth where they can stand tippy-toed, then I encourage them to lie back and float. I encourage them to experience the feeling of trusting the water to bear all their weight, all that troubles them and feels incredibly heavy. The Bible tells us to cast all our cares on God for He cares for you.

The reenactment of that scripture in this way can be very freeing. The ability in the midst of uncertainty to know that you know that God cares and you don't have to be weighted down by the cares you carry.

WHAT NOW?

Never forget living your Why is significant. Without it, the world will not be complete until you have contributed what you were created to be to it. If you rob the world of that opportunity life will be lacking all that should and could have been. Consider if the inventors of cellphones hadn't done so, or those who created airplanes gave up before it was perfected. The course of human existence would be something we couldn't recognize now.

Don't believe that your Why isn't significant.

Your Why in combination with those of our ancestors and many others in the present and to come will produce miraculous contributions in its time. Your Why has tremendous significance even if you can't see it. Don't stop honoring and living out your Why. The world awaits your creation.

NOTHING NEW UNDER THE SUN

As I write this, I know that everything written here has been said by someone else in some form or another. But if there is just one person who will read this book and find that it resonates with things they have thought about but unable to actualize, then I was created to write this book for them.

I am eternally grateful for you, whomever you are. Sharing these thoughts with you has been an honor and has fulfilled my created purpose. The events of my life have been worth it to be able to make a deposit into your life. For that, I thank you for picking up this book and reading it in its entirety.

THE DEEPEST CONTRIBUTION

All faiths and religions on some level talk about your purpose and contribution to the world. As I ponder that, I consider the seeds within an apple. When the core of an apple is discarded, the seeds within have the potential to produce thousands of apples if given the opportunity. Just one apple, just one seed can make significant contributions. With that in mind, how could you not believe your own significance, worth, contributions, and ability to effect significant change in the world?

Grains of sand individually seem insignificant but collectively they create the beaches of great bodies of water. Even on its own an individual grain of sand lodged within an oyster becomes a pearl.

You are worth much more than a thousand seeds or a thousand grains of sand.

Don't you want to find out WHY?

TO FIND OUT MORE

Janet offers a number of different services, including:

Corporate Coaching
Professional Coaching
Mentoring

To see if you're a good fit to work with Janet, scan this QR code, or visit:

https://janetpalmer.com/schedule.html

65966143R00064

Made in the USA
Columbia, SC
20 July 2019